The success of German Panzer divisions in the 1939-40 campaigns was due more to superior tactics and handling rather than superior equipment. The PzKpfw I Ausf A was typical of the light vehicles in use at this period; this one is supporting an infantry advance in Norway, April 1940.

Panzerkampfwagen

GERMAN COMBAT TANKS
1939-1945

J. Williamson

ALMARK PUBLISHING CO. LTD., LONDON

First published—June 1973

ISBN 0 85524 115 2

Printed in Great Britain by
Vale Press Ltd., Mitcham, Surrey CR4 4HR,
for the publishers, Almark Publishing Co. Ltd.,
49, Malden Way, New Malden,
Surrey KT3 6EA, England.

A PzKpfw III Ausf H parades past the divisional general who stands in front of his half-track command vehicle. The occasion is the occupation of Salonika in 1941. The small type of detachable plate with tac number is seen on this vehicle, a late example of its use—from 1940 on tac numbers were more often painted on turret sides.

Introduction

THE major German battle tanks of the Second World War and their various derivatives are probably the best documented of any military vehicles; this booklet therefore cannot claim to present any new information on the subject but it sets out to provide a basic coverage with as many photographs as possible, in line with other 'Wehrmacht Illustrated' titles.

The German tank story really started in the late 1920s when the ideas of armoured blitzkrieg tactics were being formulated. In spite of the onerous restrictions of the 1919 Versailles Treaty, secret experiments were made with prototype tanks, which the Germans more straightforwardly call Panzerkampfwagen—armoured battle vehicles. These, disguised under the commercial names of 'light' and 'heavy tractor,' were intended to act as the basis for future standard machines but it soon became obvious that development would take a long time. Meanwhile, when Hitler and the National Socialists came to power in 1933 and started to rebuild the German army, a stop-gap 'tank' was urgently needed both for propaganda

PzKpfw III Ausf E vehicles in production, probably at the Henschel works, in 1939. The nearest vehicle, however, is one of the few 'Neubaufahrzeuge' heavy tank designs, the original PzKpfw VI with 10·5 cm and 3·7 cm guns in a common mount. These saw only limited service for trials in 1940 and were then discarded.

OPPOSITE, TOP: For training purposes a turretless version of the PzKpfw I was produced. These are seen in 1939 in service with the NSKK (National Socialist Motor Corps), a para-military organisation which trained young party members for future military service. During World War 2 PzKpfw Is with turrets removed were also used as tractors and munitions carriers.

purposes and as a training device. A light armoured fighting vehicle in the 5-tonne range was therefore developed very quickly, the Krupp design being produced in 1934-5 under the rather transparent disguise of 'Landwirtschafticher Schlepper' (Industrial tractor, abbreviated to Las). Taken into service with the ordnance designation Sd Kfz 101, Panzerkampfwagen Ausführung a (ie Model A), it later became the Panzerkampfwagen I Model A (PzKpfw I Ausf A) and was quickly supplemented by an improved model, the Ausf B, with a longer hull and more powerful engine. The PzKpfw I was really only a lightly armoured machine gun carrier mounting two MG 13s but it looked most impressive in photographs and served (in decreasing numbers) as a battle tank right up to the fall of 1941. Its chassis was later used for a wide variety of purposes.

BELOW: *A field grey PzKpfw III Ausf J moving forward to the attack on the Russian Front, November, 1941. Note the national flag used as an air recognition sign for friendly aircraft.*

5

The 'workhorse' of the Panzer divisions was the PzKpfw IV which was the only German tank in production throughout the war. These Model Es are in action at Marsa El Brega during Rommel's first campaign in the Western Desert, 1941 (IWM-GR619).

By 1935 it had become obvious to General Heinz Guderian, newly appointed chief of the Panzer arm, that the 'standard' tanks would take even longer to develop than had been expected and that another stop-gap was therefore needed. The result was the Panzerkampfwagen II (abbreviated to PzKpfw II) a 7-8 tonne vehicle developed under the equally misleading code-name of 'industrial tractor 100' (LaS 100). This ran through a number of experimental versions, Ausführungen 'a' 'b' and 'c' before reaching production status in improved form as Ausf A to J. The major battle variants were all armed with a 20 mm cannon (KwK 30) and a single machine gun in a revolving turret, and the vehicle remained in front line service until late 1942 as a reconnaissance and HQ tank. It also had three interesting variants, the Models D and E which were specially produced as fast tanks with Christie suspension for the light divisions, and the Model L (later called Luchs—Lynx). This latter was built in small numbers from 1943 on as a reconnaissance vehicle to replace armoured cars. With inter-leaved roadwheels and torsion bar suspension it differed somewhat from the original PzKpfw II design.

The main 'standard' battle tanks envisaged were the famous PzKpfw III and PzKpfw IV, initially produced under the slightly less misleading disguises of 'zugführerwagen' (platoon commander's vehicle) and 'bataillonsführerwagen' (battalion commander's vehicle). The PzKpfw III was intended to be the true battle tank and, like the PzKpfw II, ran through a number of semi-experimental versions before emerging in 'standard' form as the Model E with a 3.7 cm gun in 1939. Provision had been made in the design for upgunning and the models F, G and H mounted the well-tried 50 mm cannon in its L/42 version from 1940 onwards. This, incidentally. was a tactical error and directly contrary to Hitler's own suggestion that the 50 mm L/60 version should be standard; it was not until 1941 when the tank was already proving incapable of taking on the Russian T-34 that the Model J was produced with the longer gun. Subsequently many early vehicles were re-worked with the long gun and added armour to bring them to later standards.

This L/60 gun became standard for all marks thereafter except for the Model N and some rebuilt Model Ms which mounted a short 7·5 cm low velocity gun for infantry support work. Production terminated in August 1943 in favour of assault guns on the same chassis but the basic battle tank remained in service in some quieter sections until the war's end.

The PzKpfw IV, perhaps the most successful all-round tank of the German army, had its basic features fixed with the first Model A. It was a 20/25-tonne vehicle intended originally for infantry close support and mounting a short 75 mm gun. It was initially produced only in small numbers (A-F1), and it was only 1941, when it proved capable of being radically upgunned and uparmoured, that production was concentrated on this tank to make it the standard battle tank of the Panzer Divisions. Models F2-J, armed first with the 75 mm L/43 and then with the deadly 75 mm L/48—could stand up to any western Allied tank and had a reasonable chance of success even against the Russian T-34s. They served reliably and with distinction throughout the rest of the war, and a few even survived post-war in Syrian and Spanish service until 1967 and beyond.

The T-34 tank produced by the Russians upset all the German calculations when it was encounted in the latter part of 1941 but even before its advent heavier tanks had been planned. Requirements for these were hastily

German tank strength was greatly augmented by the acquisition of Czecho-slovakian vehicles after the annexation of that country in 1939. The TNHP-S became the PzKpfw 38 (t) in German service and was one of the most advanced designs in the world at the time. This one was pictured during the invasion of France, 1940 (IWM-GER1230).

The tanks of what later became the Afrika Korps arrive in Tripoli in March 1941. Shown here, still in the field grey colour of European service, are two PzKpfw I Ausf B light tanks.

revised and they emerged in 1942-3 as the PzKpfw V Panther and the super-heavy PzKpfw VI Tiger—perhaps the most famous tanks of the war. The heavy Tiger, brought into service late in 1942 before it was really ready, ran into many teething troubles which initially made Allied Intelligence seriously underestimate its value. Once established, it proved a very form-idable opponent; the thick armour which made up most of its 56-tonne weight was almost impervious to anti-tank fire except at very short range while it mounted the deadly 8.8 cm L/56 gun, perhaps the most effective weapon of its period. The PzKpfw VI Ausführung E, or Tiger I, was produced until mid-1944 when it was succeeded by the Tiger II, or King Tiger, with a longer chassis and the even more effective 8·8 cm L/71 gun. Fortunately for the Allies this proved underpowered and mechanically unreliable and was never produced in great enough numbers to have a really serious effect.

The Panther—so named by direct order of Hitler—was potentially a very fine tank indeed. Designed with information learned from study of the T-34, it was fast, manouevrable, had very well sloped, thick armour and the very efficient 7.5 cm L/70 gun with what were, for the period, sophisticated sighting arrangements. Like the Tiger, it was rushed into service too early, in 1943 and was never really perfected. Nonetheless the Models A, D and in particular G, proved very useful battle tanks at least equal to anything the Allies produced, while there were plans for a Panther II with a smaller turret and an 88 mm gun. This never materialised; by the war's end German designers were obsessed with the idea of a super-heavy tank and were even testing out a prototype of the 190 ton Maus (Mouse) intended to mount a 15 cm gun as main armament with a 7.5 cm one as a secondary weapon. This was a design by Dr Porche, prominent among German AFV designers. A rival Ordnance Department design was the

Tiger I under construction at the Henschel factory in 1943. Compared with earlier German tanks, the Tiger was a monster, as evidenced by the relative size of the workmen fitting the turret (IWM-STT4070).

Tiger-Maus, a giant vehicle with characteristics based on the Tiger series.

Lastly should be mentioned the foreign tanks used by the Germans and one or two 'ersatz' vehicles. Most foreign vehicles including especially Italian and French designs, were used only in small numbers as the designs were in any case outmoded, but two tanks became part of the standard inventory. These were both Czech machines 'acquired' after the annexation of that country in 1939; the less important was a 1935 vintage vehicle mounting a 3.7 cm gun, the more useful was the modern (1938) design that was taken into service as the PzKpfw 38 (t). This also mounted a 3.7 cm gun with a coaxial machine gun and in 1940-1 formed a considerable proportion of German battle tank strength. Some 532 were still on strength in April 1942 and the basic chassis was in production until the war's end as a mount for self-propelled anti-tank guns (see 'Wehrmacht Illustrated' No 2 *Panzerjäger*).

The 'ersatz' vehicles were mainly of German design, and consisted of the so-called 'assault guns' (Sturmgeschützen). These were variants of basic tank chassis with a more effective gun than normal mounted in a turretless superstructure; long-barrelled versions of these on both PzKpfw III and PzKpfw IV chassis were regularly used as battle tanks by the Panzer regiments in Russia since they were quick to produce, better able to stand up to the T-34 and well suited to a defence role.

By 1944 key members of the Ordnance Department were concerned about the proliferation of models and variants being produced and the strain on production resources which were already affected by material problems. This led to the so-called 'E' series (E: Entiwicklung means universal) a projected range of complementary vehicles for the various AFV chassis all designed to use common mechanical and structural parts, thus rationalising production efforts to a great extent. Of these designs, only the huge E-100 (another super-heavy tank, in the 100-ton class) was under construction when the war ended in May, 1945. The heavy tanks in this range were derived broadly from the Tiger II/Panther II and the lighter vehicles from the PzKpfw 38 (t) series, as far as design characteristics were concerned.

Note on Designations

The normal army designation of a tank was a basic type number followed by a model (Ausführung) letter (eg, Panzerkampfwagen I, Ausführung B) In practice such designations were shortened, usually to PzKpfw, but PzKw, Pz or even Panzer—and 'Ausführung' was usually abbreviated to Ausf. There were numbers and it is, strictly speaking, inaccurate to refer to a 'Mark IV', as the British usually did. The equivalent of the 'mark' was the model letter.

Additionally, all German military purpose-built vehicles had a Sonderkraftfahrzeug (Sd Kfz) or 'special motor vehicle' designation for ordnance purposes. A single number was normally allocated to each tank type but if there was a major modification within the series it might be allocated a new Sd Kfz number (eg PzKpfw II Luchs which was regarded as a different vehicle—Sd Kfz 123 instead of Sd Kfz 121. Smaller but more radical modifications led to an addition of a further symbol to the basic number (eg, PzKpfw IV Ausf F2 with the uprated 7.5 cm gun became Sd Kfz 161/2).

Acknowledgements

Author and publisher wish to thank the Imperial War Museum (IWM), Peter Chamberlain, Axel Dückert, and Arthur North for the provision of pictures in this publication.

Mantlets

Three basic types of gun mantlet were in use, and a note may be of interest since frequent unexplained references are made to them in technical books. They were the *Walzenblende* ('dance-mount'), the conventional side mounted curved mantlet that allowed only vertical movement, the *Kugelblende* ('ball-mount'), a gimbal mounting that allowed a limited swivel movement of the barrel in any direction, and the *Saukopf* ('pigs-head') which was a streamlined shaped cover, usual over a Kugelblende. This last was used mainly in turretless vehicles but some later designs, such as the projected Panther II, had this type of mantlet.

PzKpfw I

Only 150 examples were built of the Ausführung A version of this lightly armoured machine-gun carrier. Distinguishing features were the rear mounted motor, four road wheels with external suspension bar, and the rear idler wheels at road level. Armament consisted of two 7·92 mm calibre MG 13 machine guns in a revolving turret mounted on a tall superstructure; entrance for the two man crew (driver and gunner/commander) was via a hatch in the left side and one on top of the turret. The small size is apparent by comparison with the soldier at right. See also page 1.

Definitive PzKpfw I was the Ausf B which differed mainly in having an extended rear hull to house its more powerful motor. It could easily be distinguished by its long, flat motor casing and by the 5-wheeled suspension unit with high set driving sprockets. Armament crew and access remained the same. The PzKpfw 1 Ausf B is shown on page 8.

The Kleine Panzerbefehlswagen I (small armoured command vehicle) was simply a Model B with the turret replaced by a high fixed fighting compartment, and with additional radio equipment. Armament was one forward-firing MG 13 in a gimbal mounting and access was by way of a hatch in the left side. These vehicles were not widely used but saw service principally in France and North Africa. A unit commander and signaller or staff officer could sit side by side in the fighting compartment (Arthur North).

PzKpfw II

ABOVE: Very early versions of the PzKpfw II had a turret similar to later versions but their hull design and suspension resembled more that of the

PzKpfw I. All versions mounted a 2 cm cannon and a 7·9 mm coaxial machine gun in a traversing turret but it was not until the Model c that the standard 5-wheeled torsion bar suspension unit was introduced. The earlier models, Ausf a1, a2, a3 and b had small road wheels and beam suspension and were produced in small batches in the 1935-37 period. Some were still in service in 1939-40. An Ausf b is shown.

ABOVE: The PzKpfw II Ausf B introduced the characteristic low cupola. This captured vehicle has its radio aerial trough missing from the side (IWM-MH4135). BELOW: Ausf C is shown in this builder's picture before fitting of armament and driver's armoured visor. Final 'improved' versions were the Ausf F, G and J which differed only in minor details. All had strengthened frontal armour and were produced up to 1942 mainly as re-connaisance tanks for the Regimental HQs of Panzer Regiments. The F was most common, later models being visually distinguished by the rear stowage bin on the turret.

ABOVE: Unusual variants were the Models D and E, using a standard PzKpfw II C hull and turret matched with large-wheeled Christie suspension units. These were intended for the armoured battalions of the light cavalry divisions and the Christie suspension allowed an increase of 15 km/hr in their theoretical road speed. In practice few reached the light divisions before these were converted to Panzer Divisions and most Ds and Es were converted to other uses early in their careers. Most became self-propelled guns but a few were converted to flame vehicles under the designation PzKpfw II (Flamm)—Sd Kfz 122. These served with panzer units until replaced by the equivalent version of the PzKpfw III. Vehicle in foreground in this view is a PzKpfw I Ausf A (US Official). BELOW: Final variant of the PzKpfw II was the Ausf L, later known as the Luchs (or Lynx). This was specifically a reconnaissance tank for use on the Russian front where armoured cars had proved unequal to the terrain. It was built in small numbers from 1943 on and had a much modified suspension with five large overlapping road wheels. The turret was also slightly larger, the 2 cm cannon being mounted in a full-width mantlet (IWM-STT6647).

ABOVE: *In late 1939 orders were placed with Daimler-Benz and MAN for new prototypes derived from the basic PzKpfw II design. VK 901 was a 'light' vehicle with 30 mm frontal armour. VK 1601 was a very heavy model with 80 mm frontal and 50 mm side armour Interleaved wheels with torsion bar suspension were a new feature. Small pre-production batches were built but the need for larger medium tanks meant that no production orders were placed. One of the few VK 1601s is here seen, relegated to the training role in 1943. Note prominent escape hatches in hull. The Lynx was developed by combining the best features of the VK 901 and VK 1601. BELOW: PzKpfw II Ausf B in Russia, 1941, following a PzKpfw III.*

PzKpfw III

Ausf A-D: The early PzKpfw III tanks had widely differing suspension units. mainly for experimental purposes. First ten vehicles built were designated Model A with five massive road wheels on coil springs and only two return rollers. In contrast to the changes in suspension, the basic hull and turret design was virtually unaltered in all models. The next three experimental series B, C, and D, had leaf-spring suspensions with eight small wheels similar in appearance to those of the contemporary PzKpfw IV, and had various modifications to the armouring and turret hatches. There were 15 each of Model B and C and 30 Model D, the latter featuring mechanical improvements. All were used in the Polish campaign of 1939 and some were still in service in Norway and France in 1940. The Model A is shown above and the Model D below, both in Poland.

Ausf E-G: The first full production models with the panzer regiments in 1940 were the Model E and F, with a 3·7 cm gun and the definitive suspension. This consisted of six medium-sized road wheels with torsion-bar suspension units and three return rollers at the top.

ABOVE: Model Fs in Norway, April 1940. The early vehicles had flush engine covers. For the projected 'Operation Sealion', the invasion of England in September, 1940, a number of PzKpfw III Ausf E were equipped with deep wading apparatus.

BELOW: The Ausf E and F were soon fitted, retrospectively, with the L/42 version of the 5 cm KwK gun using the same turret and mantlet. The Ausf G also appeared in 1940 and the picture shows a typical Ausf F or G as fitted with the 5 cm L/42 gun. These models featured stronger armour, of which a major sign was a single piece external mantlet. There was a storage bin at the rear of the turret and a modified commander's cupola in the later Gs. The vehicle shown has the earlier pattern cupola but the later wide spacing of the return rollers.

ABOVE: This view of a standard production PzKpfw III Ausf G shows the 5 cm gun, turret side vision ports, and the ribbed drive wheel, all characteristics of the Ausf E to G series. This particular vehicle lacks the turret stowage box but has sealing flaps for the engine cooling intakes seen raised in this view. This was one of the waterproofed vehicles earmarked but not used for amphibious operations, and a frame for a waterproof cover is visible around the hull MG mount. BELOW: Pz Bef Wg III Ausf E (previously called Ausf B) was typical of the Panzerbefehlswagen (command vehicle) conversions. Vehicle had a fixed turret with dummy wooden gun and a ball mounted MG in the right side of the mantlet. Conversion was based on the PzKpfw III Ausf E chassis. The extra radio aerials and prominent frame aerial behind turret are the main distinguishing features. Here the tank commander is signalling with semaphore batons. Other models were the Pz Bef Wg III Ausf A, and Pz Bef Wg III Ausf H, both basically similar externally except for chassis details.

*Ausf J-M: Most effective battle tank version of PzKpfw III was un-
doubtedly the Ausf J, produced in 1941, initially with the 5 cm L/42 gun
and armour increased to 50 mm in the most important places. Later vehicles
had the improved L/60 gun. The very similar Ausf L and M models had
the 5 cm L/60 gun and all three models had additional spaced armour in
front of the superstructure. The Ausf J (below) shows the spaced armour
plus sandbags and track shoes for added nose protection. Wider tracks
and new pattern idlers and sprockets came in with the earlier Ausf H.
The Ausf L (above) shows the longer L/60 5 cm gun, spaced armour on
mantlet and armoured louvres on the engine covers.*

ABOVE: *The Ausf K designation was reserved for the final model of command vehicle and was actually a BfPzWg III Ausf K. Unlike earlier Panzerbefehlswagen, the Ausf K had the normal tank armament but carried extra radio equipment. This one has the L/60 gun and an additional aerial behind the turret. This vehicle has an early pattern driving wheel and could well be an old model refurbished as an Ausf K. However, the skirt armour on hull and turret also representative of the almost identical PzKpfw III Ausf M. On this model the hull side escape hatches and turret vision ports were eliminated to simplify production. Barely distinguishable from the normal M series tank was the PzKpfw III (Flamm), armed with a flame-thrower in place of the 5 cm gun. The thrower was mounted in the ordinary turret and the long barret much resemble the original main armament although the mantlet was more massive. BELOW: The final version was the Ausf N mounting a short 7·5 cm L/24 gun. Thus, ironically, what had been the main battle tank took over the role of an infantry support weapon; it was issued to Panzer Grenadier divisions for this purpose from late 1942 on. Note the slightly strengthened suspension units fore and aft*
(Axel Dückert).

PzKpfw IV

ABOVE: The first production model of the PzKpfw IV, the Ausf A, set the basic pattern for hull and suspension which continued in all models. The eight small road wheels, sprung in pairs, with four return rollers and a low-set driving sprocket were characteristic of all variants as was the general turret shape. Armament was the 7·5 cm L/24 gun and the vehicle was intended as a support tank. Only 35 were built. Note the dustbin type cupola (turret is traversed) with vision slits. Note also the stepped super-structure front. BELOW: The Ausf D was built in quantity for issue to the heavy companies of panzer units. Externally very similar it had an uprated motor and thicker armour, particularly in front of the driver's compartment.

ABOVE: *The Model D (last page) introduced an external mantlet and had a staggered front superstructure with the driver slightly forward of the hull machine gunner (as in the Model A). The earlier Ausf B and C differed in having a straight superstructure front, as is well shown in this view of a PzKpfw IV Ausf C in Flanders during May, 1940. Models B and C were built in 1937-38, a total of less than 200. A more, powerful engine, new armoured cupola, thicker front armour, and elimination of the hull front machine gun were distinctive features.* BELOW: *By contrast the Ausf E, introduced in late 1939, had a new lower, thicker cupola, sited further forward in the burret roof. A venting cowl was added in the turret roof (just visible here in front of the cupola). The superstructure front was retained as in the D, but staggered extra armour plates were riveted on. A simpler style of drive sprocket was also adopted (Chamberlain collection).*

The PzKpfw IV Ausf F2 was essentially similar so far as hull and armour were concerned but mounted the L/43 high velocity 7·5 cm gun in a modified turret. This was the first really effective battle-tank version and appeared in 1942. It represented an attempt to meet the fire-power of the T-34 on the Russian Front and gave the Afrika Korps superiority in the Western Desert. BELOW: An early F2 with single baffle muzzle brake. BOTTOM: Later F2 with double baffle muzzle brake. Later versions of the PzKpfw IV, especially the H and J machines which became standard later in the war, had longer L/48 guns and were externally very similar to each other.

ABOVE: This H model shows the characteristic armour skirts (Schurzen) applied to turret (and hull) sides on these machines as a protection against hollow-charge projectiles. The flimsy 5 mm thick plates were intended only to detonate missiles prematurely and often got damaged or torn off in the stress of battle. BELOW: The Model J did not have full skirts since steel was in short supply by 1944 and even wire mesh would detonate the missile. Like the Ausf H it had the 7·5 cm L/48 gun and, typically, spare bogie wheels stored two by two in racks at each side of the hull. Model J had extra internal fuel tanks replacing the power traverse gear. There was also a new exhaust system.

ABOVE: This top view of a PzKpfw IV Ausf H shows exactly how the supplementary skirt armour was arranged round the hull and turret, held by rails and supports. Driver's and wireless operator's hatches are shown open. The Ausf H and J were 1943-44 production models, the J remaining in service until the war's end. BELOW: PzKpfw IV Ausf G was in essence a refined F2. It had thicker turret roof armour (15 mm) and turret side vision ports were omitted (Chamberlain collection).

NbFz, PzKpfw V and VI

When the PzKpfw III and IV were designed in the mid-1930s, they were supplemented by a third design for the heavy tank, role. This was the neubaufahrzeuge ('new construction'—Nb Fz), built with different armaments and originally and PzKpfw VI (10·5 cm and 3·7 cm guns). Two small auxiliary turrets carried MGs. The design was typical of other nations' heavy tanks; only about six examples were built (and used in 1940) after which the type was discontinued and the later Panther and Tiger took the designations.

PzKpfw Maus

Maus was designed by Porsche to meet Hitler's idea for a huge 100 ton tank. When conceived early in 1942 it was code-named Mammoth (Mammut). The vehicle had electric drive with a petrol (later diesel) engine mounted forward in the hull. Armour maximum was 240 mm, planned armament being a 15 cm L/38 gun and a 7·5 cm gun. As finished, the prototype weighed 188 tons. Too heavy for bridges, it was submersible to 24 ft, specially for crossing rivers. Only two prototypes were nearly ready when the war ended; the first of them is shown below on trials. The design was, however fairly impractical by any standards.

PzKpfw VI Ausf E, Tiger I

The famous Tiger tank was designed in 1941 and prototypes were ready by April, 1942. A Porsche design with petrol-electric drive was not selected for production but Henschel's rival model had conventional drive and was more suited for use. The requirement evolved from various ideas for a 'heavy break-through tank' dating back to 1937. The eventual specification called for a 45 ton vehicle with the heaviest possible gun—an adaptation of the 8·8 cm AA gun. The design appeared before the great virtues of the Russian T-34 were fully appreciated. The Tiger emerged as a thoroughly engineered vehicle with 100 mm armour welded and slotted together, wide 'battle' tracks or narrower 'road' tracks, and interleaved wheel suspension. ABOVE: Early models saw action in late 1942 and early in 1943 were used in Tunis. This one has its 'snorkel' breathing tube erected, with elaborate waterproofing, a feature of the early vehicles (IWM-STT3597). BELOW: Late production models omitted the 'snorkel' and waterproofing, also the air filters, and had all steel wheels instead of the earlier rubber tyred type. They also had narrow tracks only (IWM-NA17525).

ABOVE: An impressive front view of the Tiger I showing the very wide tracks and the side panniers of the superstructure overhanging the track. This allowed a large diameter turret and hence a big gun. BELOW: A sand coloured PzKpfw V Panther leaving the factory, with Tiger tanks behind. The Panther shown is the Ausf D Model with early type cupola, and hull side skirts. Note visor hatch for driver and slit for machine gunner on nose.

PzKpfw V, Panther

The Panther was the most successful and effective of the German tanks. It was designed in direct response to the appearance of the Soviet T-34, the latter being superior to all previous German designs. The Panther was designed in 1942, and several T-34 features were incorporated, notably the sloped hull faces, panniers overhanging the tracks, and wide track shoes. Priority production facilities ensured that the first vehicles were ready in November, 1942 with major production starting in several plants early in 1943. Over 4,800 were built by the war's end and there was also a Jagdpanther tank destroyer and a recovery vehicle conversion. Front armour was over 100 mm and top speed over 30 mph.

ABOVE: First production model was actually the Ausf D. This view shows the large, overlapping road wheels and broad tracks that gave the tank such a good cross-country performance. Also notable is the very long 7·5 cm gun. Extra aerials denote this as a command vehicle, Bf Pz Wg Panther. There was also an observation post vehicle with short dummy gun. BELOW: Best operational version was the Model G, which featured a redesigned hull having unbroken slope on the side armour, and an improved commander's cupola with prismatic vision slits all round. It had a ball-mounted front MG. Some vehicles were fitted with smoke dischargers on the turret. Captured vehicle is shown. Interim model was Ausf A with ball mounted front MG, new cupola, but earlier style of hull shape.

PzKpfw VI Ausf B, Tiger II

Two versions of the much heavier (76 tonne) Tiger II Ausf B were produced, as a result of another requirement for which both Henschel and Porsche submitted designs. The Henschel hull form was adopted, but the first fifty vehicles utilised Porsche turrets built in anticipation of a contract. This view shows clearly the more angular Henschel production turret, with a kugelblende mantlet for the 8·8 cm L/71 gun. A projected similar vehicle was the Panther II which would have many parts in common with the Tiger II. However, this vehicle was not produced before the war ended.

Captured types in German service

Shown here are some of the more common captured types which saw regular service with the German forces. Many more types of tank saw service of a more temporary nature when captured and used only in a particular battle or campaign.

PzKpfw 35 (t): Characteristic features of this Czech-built tank were the vulnerable suspension units and the old fashioned rivetted superstructure with its prominent turret cupola. It was used in some numbers during the French campaign of 1940 by 6th Panzer Division and later by the Rumanian and Hungarian armies. It was a reliable and well-liked vehicle

PzKpfw 38 (t): Much more modern though still of rivetted construction was the Czech-built PzKpfw 38 (t). An excellent, robust and fast vehicle, it formed a good part of German strength during the 1940 campaigns and did not disappear as a battle tank until the end of 1941. The very good chassis was used for self-propelled gun conversions right up to the war's end. Unlike German tanks, it had a right hand drive, the hull machine gun in a gimbal mounting being placed just left of centre. Another view of the PzKpfw 38 (t) is given on page 7 (IWM-MH9217).

BELOW: Many captured French vehicles were used for internal security work in Europe—some even served on the Russian Front. Shown here is a Somua leading a Hotchkiss H39/40 on a Luftwaffe airfield patrol in France, 1941.

PRINCIPAL TANK DESIGNS: BASIC SPECIFICATIONS

VEHICLE (and model)	ORD DESIG.	LENGTH OVER HULL (Metres)	WIDTH (metres)	HEIGHT (metres)	BATTLE WT (Tonnes)	THICKEST ARMOUR (mm)	ENGINE	H.P.	MAX. SPEED X-COUNTRY kph	MAX. RANGE (km)	MAIN ARMAMENT	MACHINE GUNS
PzKpfw 1 Ausf A.	SdKfz 101	4.02	2.06	1.72	5.4	13	KRUPP M305 4 cyl	57	37	145	2xMG13	
PzKpfw 1 Ausf B	,,	4.42	2.06	1.72	6.0	13	MAYBACH NL38TR 6 cyl.	100	40	140	,,	
KI Pz Bef Wg (PzKpfw 1)	SdKfz 265	4.42	2.06	1.72	5.9	14.5	MAYBACH NL38TR 6 cyl.	100	40	170	1xMG13	
PzKpfw II Ausf C	SdKfz 121	4.81	2.24	1.98	9.5	15	MAYBACH HL62TRM 6 cyl.	140	19	200	2cm KwK 30	1
Ausf D/E	,,	4.64	2.30	2.02	10.0	30	MAYBACH HL62TRM 6 cyl.	140	19	200	,,	1
Ausf F-J	,,	4.81	2.28	1.98	9.5	35	MAYBACH HL62TRM 6 cyl.	140	19	200	2cm KwK 38	1
PzKpfw Luchs	SdKfz 123	4.63	2.49	2.13	11.8	30	MAYBACH HL66P 6 cyl.	180	N/K	250	,,	1
PzKpfw III Ausf D	SdKfz 141	5.41	2.91	2.44	19.3	30	MAYBACH HL120TR 12 cyl.	320	N/K	165	3.7cm KwK L/45	2
Ausf E	,,	5.41	2.91	2.44	19.5	30	MAYBACH HL120TRM 12 cyl.	300	18	175	5cm KwK L/42	2
Ausf F/G	,,	5.41	2.91	2.44	20.3	30	MAYBACH HL120TRM 12 cyl.	300	18	175	,,	2
Ausf J-N	,,	5.52	2.95	2.50	22.3	50	MAYBACH HL120TRM 12 cyl.	300	18	175	5cm KwK L/60 (J-M) 7.5cm KwK L/24 (M+N)	2 2
PzKpfw IV Ausf A	SdKfz 161	5.60	2.85	2.59	17.3	14.5	MAYBACH HL108TR 12 cyl.	250	17	150	7.5cm KwK L/24	2
Ausf D	,,	5.91	2.85	2.68	20.0	30	MAYBACH HL120TRM 12 cyl.	300	20	200	,,	2
Ausf F1	,,	5.93	2.88	2.68	22.3	50	MAYBACH HL120TRM 12 cyl.	300	20	200	,,	2
Ausf F2	,,	,,	,,	,,	23.6	50	MAYBACH HL120TRM 12 cyl.	300	16	200	7.5cm KwK L/43	2
Ausf G	SdKfz 161/1	5.91	2.88†	2.68	23.6	50	MAYBACH HL120TRM 12 cyl.	300	16	200	7.5cm KwK L/43	2
H/J	SdKfz 161/2	5.89	2.88†	2.68	25.0	80	MAYBACH HL120TRM 12 cyl.	300	16	2.300	7.5cm KwK L/48	2
PzKpfw Panther D	SdKfz 171	6.88	3.43	2.95	43.0	80	MAYBACH HL210 P30 12 cyl.	650	24	c170	7.5cm KwK L/70	2·3
A/G	,,	6.88	3.43	3.00	44.8 45.5	80	MAYBACH HL210 P30 12 cyl.	700	24	c170	,,	2·3
PzKpfw Tiger Ausf E	SdKfz 189	6.20	3.73*	2.86	55.0	100	MAYBACH HL230 P45 12 cyl.	700	20	c100	88cm KwK L/56	2
Ausf B	182	7.26	3.75†	3.09	69.7	150	MAYBACH HL230 P30 12 cyl.	700	17	c100	88cm KwK L/71	2
PzKpfw 35 (t)	—	4.45	2.14	2.20	10.5	25	SKODA TII 4 cyl.	120	N/K	190	3.7 KwK L/40 (t)	2
PzKpfw 38 (t)	—	4.90	2.06	2.37	c9.73	25	PRAGA EPA 6 cyl.	125	15	230	3.7 KwK L/40 (t) or 3.7 KwK L/45	2
PzKpfw Maus	—	9.03	3.67	3.66	c1.90	200	DAIMLER-BENZ MB509 12 cyl.	1200	N/K	c190	—	

†without skirting
*with fighting tracks